THE MOT

To f

Tom
May 96.

THE MOTH TRAP

TOM POW

with wood engravings by Jonathan Gibbs

CANONGATE

First published in 1990
by Canongate Publishing Limited
17 Jeffrey Street, Edinburgh, Scotland

© 1990 Tom Pow
© wood engravings 1990 Jonathan Gibbs

British Library Cataloguing in Publication Data
Pow, Tom
The Moth Trap
I. Title
821'.914
ISBN 0-86241-299-4

The publishers acknowledge the financial assistance
of the Scottish Arts Council
towards the publication of this volume

Typeset by Speedspools, Edinburgh
Printed and bound by Norhaven, S.A., Viborg, Denmark

For my sister –
Katherine

Acknowledgements

Some of these first appeared in *Chapman, New Writing Scotland VI, Rubicon* (Montreal), *South Coast Poetry Journal* (California). *Galloway Tale* and *Russian Still Life* were first published in the *New Yorker. One Afternoon in Early Summer* was commissioned by *The Glasgow Herald,* as part of its New Writing feature. *In Old Galloway* first appeared as a poster produced by Book Trust (Scotland).

I would like to acknowledge my debt to Annie Dilliard's *Pilgrim at Tinker's Creek.* Her account (in the chapter *Seeing*) of the experiences of those who have had their sight restored was invaluable in the composition of part one of *The Gift of Sight,* and the genesis of *Galloway Tale,* I owe to Frank Farrell. The glass-plate slides of *Gala Day – Castle Douglas 1909* were taken by R. L. Collin, about when little is known, and are in the keeping of the Rev. Holland of New Abbey.

I would like to thank the Scottish Arts Council and Dumfries and Galloway Education Authority for enabling me to take the time to complete this book.

Contents

Summer Haiku   1

SECTION ONE

In Old Galloway   5
Ghosts I   6
Ghosts II   8
The Trader   9
The Death of Mark Robert Smith   12
Galloway Tale   16
The Gift of Sight
  Part One : Kirkmaiden   18
  Part Two : Saint Medan   22
Elegy for an SS20   25
Gala Day – Castle Douglas 1909   27
At Cairnholy   28

SECTION TWO

One Afternoon in Early Summer
  1. The Visitation (Jacob Epstein)   30
  2. The King and Queen   32
  3. Dry Stane Dyke   34
  4. Routin Linn   36
  5. The Twelve Apostles   38

SECTION THREE

The Moth Trap   43
Portrait (Aged 6) : Inverleith Park Pond   44
Snap   50
Once I Knew You   51
Frogs   53
First Rites   55
The Flower   57
The Moth   60

The Foxglove   62
Message   67
Casey's   68
On Arran   70
On Saddleworth   72

SECTION FOUR

Visiting the Poet   75
The Children of the Russian Fair   76
Russian Still-life   78
Kissing a Hand in Checkhov   79

Summer Haiku

a couple of beasts
at water – the wolf
children of Tiree.

SECTION ONE

In Old Galloway

Turf was torn from rich earth
and laid on poor ; a wealth
of dykes conjured up
the steepest slopes – till a green
democracy was everywhere.

On bright summer evenings,
grasslands lit from within,
where would a child not go ?
Up the hawthorns, over the hill
to Away ! Of course, it's a lie :

this land too is rucked
with the bones and blood
guide books never chart.
In early spring, we pluck
little white knuckles from rich
dark moss – the kind that lines
the more comfortable
contours of our hearts.

Ghosts I

(The upholding of the right in question was documented in 1726.)

Remember I told you
of the ancient right
once claimed by the sparling fishers
of Minnigaff – that during the fishing
they may sleep in the bed
in the farm kitchen of Machermore
with whatever woman is there ; the woman
being unclothed and no indecency
being committed.

Well, it gave me ideas
for insomnia. Now I have
a burgeoning night-time career.

No more for me memory's frozen rump ;
no more thrashing in the white wilderness –
it is not a way to sleep
or to live. I prefer the warmth
of a stranger's bed.

Perhaps lately you have felt
my presence with you ? –

though I have learned poise, stealth,
the value of stillness so well,
I can slip between the sheets
without the hint of a draught
touching you.

I like to feel a breathing body
next to mine : the heart pumping,
blood moving, the lungs
receiving, sending blood forth
transformed . . .

I am not alone
in liking to share such movements –

though they may seem
insubstantial to you ;
ghostly as the flounder-trampers
we watched that summer evening
from high on the grassy fort.
Children they were, far out
on the unbroken fields of sand.

Remember I told you
they were the ghosts
of drowned fishermen
and that night you woke in panic,
your heart in the despairing clutch
of cold, rough, absent hands.

Ghosts II

'It's like dung in the teeth of my lover:
the knowledge that each night I must cower
in this small bed, while a stranger lowers
himself down and tugs at the covers.

It's then I feel the rough cloth stiffen
my nipples – this, the first stolen gift –
and, as a membrane between us, graft
together hearts that are barely living.

Yet *his* salt-heart still pumps like bellows
the slow blood's tired passage to his lungs;
and with it, all I've held precious flows
into a midden of corrupted song.

Pet farm-dogs twitch now by the dying fire
and the world shrinks within four thick walls.
I listen to the winds bind Machermore
to a darkness tighter than any laws.

From a grassy hill once, I watched ghosts –
flounder-trampers, far out on fields of sand.
They come to me now like fishermen lost
in the waters of sleep they fear most.

It's from such desperate hands I turn;
from a language I'd rather not learn.
But lover be quick! My body is milk
souring in a tall, cold churn.'

The Trader

'October 3rd (1831), when the disease (Cholera) reached its culminating stage, was market-day; but when death was mercilessly tithing the town, no business toll was levied at the bridge. Out of nearly sixty carriers only one made his appearance.' (McDowell's History of Dumfries.)

I

Never could he forget that day
(the innocent beginnings
like rituals, unquestioned
as breath) when he crossed
the hump-backed bridge, his produce
no longer heavy on his back.
From the brow of the hill
he'd looked on the town
as an oil-board panorama
two thirds sky –
a badly-weathered sky
whose varnish had been too thick
and darkening had gone hand-in-hand
with time's quotidian cracks.
This was the first omen
of ill: 'a dull, heavy film
altered the sun's rays
from bright gold to a lurid orange
mantling the town
in its shadow.' Such that
at the foot of the board –
equally dark – on the scroll
of the river might be written:
*Watch therefore for ye know
neither the day nor the hour.*

Even in old age
he terrified children
talking of the Great Pestilence ;
for each simple brush stroke
remained separate and clear :
a dab of white –
a dead gull's wing, floating
down the river.
                    And yet
he could never explain
what had made him
walk towards that silence,
inhabit that darkness
in the tight fist of the town,
where air was rank
with the thick black smoke
of burning tar and pitch ;
where everyone's nightmare
was the croak of *vox
cholerica* – the dusky-blue tinge
of death ; where between cracked voices
there was even relish
for the equalising power
of death.

Years later they said
water was to blame –
that the river, swollen
with mud and refuse had quenched
yet contaminated the whole town.
But sweet reason
could not account
that he came back
a changed man – as if
something in himself
had been confirmed
and he knew time
would never shift it.

Thereafter, on all his travels,
what he liked best
was not travelling, not arriving,
but finding a small space
on a coach, a cabin, a chair –
a hard-fought space – where

II

in the half-dark of a chill autumn morning,
the early ground still pocked with mist

a young man is wiping tiny feathers
stuck with shit from warm brown eggs

placing each egg carefully between
layers of golden straw. And these

are movements there is no leaving
(the casual wave to his wife, framed

in the kitchen door), movements
that require the utmost concentration

for he must not break a single one;
movements that in the endless

repeating – over and over and over –
attain the forgetful purity of prayer.

The Death Mask of Robert Smith

(Dumfries Museum. Hanged in Dumfries 12/5/1868 – the last public execution in Scotland. Askern was the hangman.)

'There's no art/ To find the mind's construction in the face.'
Macbeth – Shakespeare.

I

Not sleep. Neither the brief, fugitive sleep
of Cain, nor that from which his warders
could barely shake him. More like the moment
a head's dragged up out of water, when hair's
plastered back, eyes blind, lips ready for breath.
His are lop-sided – sign of a final,
choking drool; for Askern the dandy – dressed
more for a wedding than hanging – has bungled.
The head itself is narrow and the features
so ordinary – the small ears pinched in
at the top, nose just slightly off-centre –
it's a landscape with next to no bearings.
Nothing to draw from us a purity
of hatred or anger – even pity.
Pity for him? Nineteen and stocky-strong,
he coaxed Thomasina Scott (eleven)
into the dismal firs of Crofthead Wood;
raped her, strangled her, stole from her the clutch
of coins she'd been given for messages.
We stare, but the head stays a mildewed map,
washed by light – yielding nothing. And again,
it seems, we're stumbling around in the dark.

II

This evening
on the train, as light
fades and fields,
roads, houses
meld into blackness,
I pass
the dark arm
of Crofthead
Woods and think
of this again.
Sticks beat
through trees
the Sabbath
after the murder –
another cold,
winter's day.
Wind whipped in
from the Solway
across flat,
fallow fields.
Horses brushed
dry twigs
aside ; shouts
rang out,
as scores of men,
women and children,
set free
from worship
after one short,
earth-bound
prayer, chased
the chill from the day,
smelled the hunt,
were scoured
by their own fear.

III

And the same Sabbath morning, *he* is found
at Kirk's Lodging House, Dumfries, enjoying
a pipe of tobacco, coolly dandling

a favourite child on his knee: Tell me,
what does all this clumsiness mean? His trail,
not so much clues as signposts –

the knees of his britches still bloody,
his naked wrists scratched; in his pocket
a handkerchief 'wet with blood' they tell it

as if a horrified Nature had foregone its laws?
Does he see these damp walls as his Gethsemane? –
while back there – fifteen short miles –

they chip bits from the tree where she was found,
as if it is the Devil's Rood or next best thing
to chipping out his hazel eyes.

Do you know, in the dim lantern light,
to begin with, they could not tell
what had killed her? Shock –

or loss of all the thick, dark blood
that glazed her frozen thighs,
that clotted her hairless slit.

IV

Then it was, sometime after his 'full
and free confession', that they almost came
to love him : Robert Smith, orphan, bastard,

homeless, loveless, neither knower nor giver
of excuses for his muck of a life. A man drunk
on all he'd dreamed of evil, writing now

to the witness whose throat he'd tried to slit,
'Give my kind love to all the neighbours,
to your son John and to all the broom men ;

and tell them that I will not see none of them
on earth, but I trust God I will see you
and yours and them in heaven.'

V

Come May – a wet dismal morning – up against
the barricades in Buccleuch Street,

many of the six hundred turn their backs
and run. Those who stay,

sigh deeply at each sorry stage
of ritual. But those who – at the last –

cut him dowm, after he has choked and kicked
for fully nine minutes (Askern, you bastard);

those who get close, as we can, must see
that for him – if not for you, if not for me –

Death is some kind of Baptism. Robert Smith
no more, they carry him shamelessly in their arms.

Galloway Tale

He told the map men anything.
But in Gaelic. That stretch
of bog? Old woman's fanny.
The small rise? Mharie's tit.

The maps were all printed
before he was rumbled: an ageing
hill shepherd – what did he
want of the outside world?

Provisions perhaps. Tools. A wife.
Each market day for two years
he wooed her (his fistfuls
of violets bound up with wool),

till – drunk as a lord –
after the market, after the wedding,
he took her back to the bald hills,
the gurgling-sounding places.

Years later, children were seen,
fetching water from dark pools,
cupping curlews' eggs. It's said
they fixed you with brown eyes,

sharp as kestrels', hovered
momentarily – and were gone
behind a line of dogs conjured
from the green ruff around

the thick-walled bothy. A slum
in the heather – so some saw it –
black pans lying unscoured, ropes
of washing rotting in damp piles.

When she died, he carried her
over the hills, over the burns
on his back. At her graveside,
in the rain, he mourned on alone,

while in the pub, they put on
prim cartographer faces
and muttered that the loneliness
of earth would suit her.

The Gift of Sight

PART ONE : KIRKMAIDEN

(Chapel on the Wigton coast, dedicated to the Irish Saint Medan. There is a well associated with her on the foreshore, which was believed to possess miraculous curative powers for the blind.)

I

How many have noted the earth steps give
beneath their feet; or the November air,
between motes of salt-crystal, alive
with darting bird-song? Or sensed cliff-shelter
as a shawl around them, distance as time
behind them – or could know this rock beneath me
is the last thing with which I'll truly rhyme?
Resting one hand on its roughness, sets free
the other to dip into the healing spring.

The water is so heavy, the first time
I cannot lift it to my face. I sink
to my knees and cast the last of my blind
shadows on the damp earth. For one moment
more, I want to float in the world's warm womb,
sensing all things connect as membranes sent
to touch me. I fear an airier room.

II

This new world is light!
A pure geometry of sand, sea and sky:
a frieze of wings caught in quivering flight.
The sea, stippled with silver, is beauty
so achingly bright, I can barely look
into the sweep of the bay. But my heart
leaps; I choke. A dog on a chain, I seek
freedom in the field of light, yet the part
that should give it – the eyes – can only run,
headless and hopeless, over what befalls them,
unable to find one spot, as my true hand
had that lichened rock, on which to rest. Then –

I want to tear at the air; unstitch sound
and smell – from bird, bracken and earth – let
the compass of the world, once more, be found
within what my body desired and felt.

I throw a stone before me, as I measure
my way across the smooth sand to the sea.
I stretch out my hands to the sky's fissure,
but even the skerries are beyond me.

III

How can I say now what I expected?
They had told me I missed so much.
But there is a world I miss now, wrecked
beyond repair. Its peace was not a crutch,
but the whole, full sail of it. Now the wind
falls from it as each sighted day goes past.
A cup, a handle, a lid's rusted hinge:
I trust only what these two hands can grasp;
surer than a world of dull appearance,
where distance form and size are only coarse,
meaningless syllables – lies. Ignorance
was my serenity: *I* was the source
of my inner spring. But this water – so cool

in cupped hand – scalded my eyes and heart
in the healing. Now I'm learning the rules
of this new world; its make-up – equal parts
beauty and terror.
                              Below the curtain
of blue-grey light, the fountain was ringed
by a tight knit of bramble and bracken.
The first colour-patch I saw was winged
and singing a hymn to itself; sitting
on a spiked hoop – a robin's red tongue.

It told me there is too much to grieve for,
too much deserving praise in this lit world;
that the spikes of the bramble and the gore
of its flaming breast appear in a whorl
of images more fitting to a template
of the world than the ethereal curtain
of light. In the mirror now, what I hate
isn't my own certain dissolution,
but all the ghosts I carry in my eyes:
too much evidence of death and dying.
(Look, how with their carpets of sores, they rise
from each rheumy universe; each vying
for his own sad attentions.) And now,
that the helping hand has left me – the bread,
the coin, the trite word that feeling allowed –
I see how much I am of this world. And fed
on what is earthy, physical, debased,
I see what a prize beauty is. The cause
of that leaping, choking heart – chased
more than gold – can be borne as a curse.

PART TWO : SAINT MEDAN

That Medan was beautiful,
    there was no doubt.
Wherever she went,
    hearts were routed.

But, to her, these looks
    were but a costume
she couldn't cast off.
    She saw her fortune

not in the fancy
    of romantic play –
it was in inner things
    her interests lay.

Medan took a vow
    of chastity ; her life
she bound to Christ.
    It was a sharp knife

in the hearts of men.
    But one noble knight
did not believe her.
    To quit his sight

she left Ireland
    for green Galloway.
To the Rhins she came,
    to live in poverty.

The knight followed.
    He would die or wed
his heart's crusade.
    Pure Medan now fled

to a rock in the sea.
　　　　With prayer, the rock
became a boat ;
　　　　the boat she took

thirty miles away.
　　　　Still, he followed ;
blindly obeying
　　　　what the hollow

in his heart called for.
　　　　He'd have been lost,
but a crowing cock –
　　　　to both their costs –

told him the house
　　　　where Medan lay.
Shaken, she climbed
　　　　and she prayed

as she climbed
　　　　into a thorn tree.
From there, she asked,
　　　　'What do you see

in me to excite
　　　　your passion ?' 'Your face
and eyes,' he replied.
　　　　She sighed, 'In which case . . .'

then impaled her eyes
　　　　on two sharp thorns
and flung them at him.
　　　　Desire was torn

forever from that knight.
　　　　He looked at his feet,
where the eyes had rolled –
　　　　lustrous jade, now meat

for ants. Horror-struck,
    he left – a penitent.
Medan washed her face,
    for a spring – heaven-sent –

gurgled from the dry earth.
    The rest of her days
were lived in poverty
    and sanctity. (*Praise*

the Lord, sang Ninian.)
    The proud cock half-lived,
but crowed no more.
    And sight became the gift

Saint Medan gave,
    so that all could suffer
in equal measure,
    beauty and terror.

Elegy for an SS20

*(Luce Bay: base for airship defence of shipping in the Irish Sea
– 1915–18. The SS20 was the most up-to-date airship used. It
recorded no hits.)*

The evening sun ignites the grass-heads
and highlights the riffling leaves in a bed
of turnips. Dipping beneath a beehive stack
of the thickest white cloud, each segment breaks
into a silver shower on the grey sea
and the whole deep bay is suddenly
transformed into a glowing cave of light.
Shielding my eyes from the sun, I catch sight

of the last SS20 coming home.
A monstrous bird, its blunted edges comb
through trailing wisps of cloud, but its motor's birr
barely gives the air more stir
than the gentlest shore-slap of the sea.
Snug in his gondola, the Commander reads ·
the complex gossip of the wind and pulls
at various wheels and levers until

the airship turns ; moving – neither agile
nor innocent – with a dinosaur's guile.
Below him the Siamese hammerhead
of the Mull holds all together : the bread
of its fields, its cliff-edges fringed with white,
the clear needle of the lighthouse – a bright
pointer to home. Once more his bombs
have dropped harmlessly, his known sum

of damage is none. Yet – Ardberg, Ben Rein,
Conningsberg, Chirripo – the line
stretches as *Metal Sharks Roam the Deep*
spreading terror and the lost tonnage seeps
into history. (Each ascension cloud,
with feathered top ablaze, on the green mounds
of Wigtown is a memorial to those
whose bones are found where the Gulf Stream flows.)

And this death-map matches the ancient routes
that Ninian and his followers took
to this softly-contoured land; to demand
that scattered tribes – swords held in calloused hands –
should bend to their fierce disciplines of love.
I watch the darkening sky far above
their markings – Petrus, Latinus, Monreith Cross –
till behind great carved clouds, my ship is lost.

Gala Day – Castle Douglas 1909

*(Seeing glassplate photographs of the second year the balloonist
came, an old woman remembers.)*

Yes, the special excitement of that day
in a small, provincial Scottish town.
Sunday-suited men, ladies dressed for May ;
gold chains and bonnets shining in the sun.

Slowly the balloon filled like a huge ear
of corn. It fattened. It will fill the sky !
The Grand Hotel's behind it now. No fear –
this year, surely, we will see it fly.

A wayard spark ? A weakness in a seam ?
A torn flag hangs in heavy, summer air.
Adults stand transfixed by thick, black streams
of smoke. In the corner, there's a white blur :

that's me, running off – halfpenny tight-shut
in hand – the year I hit my coconut.

At Cairnholy

(Chambered cairn: third millennia B.C.)

The Cairnholy sun
dyed the cold sky red,
dispensed with forests;
made sea echo stone.
For, in winter, Wigtown
deals elements; lead
us, like lapsed priests,
to its burial homes.

On a court of dead grass,
before a facade
of chiselled pillars,
we lit two sparklers
against the black mass
of night. As darkness bled
around our shelter,
we made a mark there

with a brief ritual
of laughter and light.
Two innocent fires
circle each other.
They spark off nuptuals –
like moths, each one light
to the other – till tired
dancing, they wither.

The ceremony
burns still; a small fire
in my distant heart.
Though bones stand on bones,
our truest story
is told by frail wires
of ash, the colour
of Cairnholy stone.

SECTION TWO

ONE AFTERNOON IN EARLY SUMMER

TO THE READER

To this necklace of locations
a few winding miles from where I live,
if you were my friend and I your guide,
then this is the tour that I'd give.

1. The Visitation (Jacob Epstein)

In her presence, a glance
is enough for quiet.
Young woman in a trance,
she looks down but not at

the particular : here,
cropped grass, a scattering
of daffodils – the floor
of an ancient pine ring

in which she's found shelter.
And if a needle or cone,
from its spiked canopy,
should, with the softest moan,

fall on her neck – the nape
of it bared by pig-tails ;
not the light ones of girl-hood,
nor yet the heavy coils

of age – she would not look up,
more than she hauls her shawl
over that tender spot
when, in winter, snow falls

from the thick combs of pine.
But if, in pity, you tug
her wrist, gently begin
to say, 'Now come, enough –

away,' it would spring back
to cover the other,
as if they'd grown like that ;
one hand brother, sister,

mother to the other –
kin in a world of thorns
beyond her belly's growth.
As if the secret bond

between her hands was all
there was ever to say
and her heavy eyes still
look past them – and away.

2. The King and Queen

Of course, the proper time to see the King and Queen by Henry Moore, the most famous of the Glenkiln statues, situated on a gentle hillside overlooking the loch, is in autumn or winter ; snow or rain – it doesn't matter : the responsibility of power will move you.

Consider how the King, his Queen by his side on their benchlike throne, bear witness to their bedraggled kingdom, as the watery elements gather in their laps. (A bonus, the hawthorn ; thorny crowning of the hilltop behind them – so photogenic, so theatrical !)

. . . .

But of course, the proper time to see the King and Queen by Henry Moore is in spring or summer. To see them, burnished by sunlight, against a clear sky (that hawthorn in bloom) is an airier, lighter pleasure.

For now a lightness, a playfulness is to be seen. Have not this King and Queen just climbed the gentle slope before us ? And now they rest on this simple bench, as they look over their kingdom – blue loch, purple hill, fishermen, wildlife – and see that it is good.

. . . .

Of course, Henry Moore knew, when he allowed the statue to be removed from London during the Blitz, that the proper time to see his King and Queen is now.

Consider the fugitive couple, plucked from the burning world, their birdlike skulls a store for such nightmares, they must see through the seasons without sleep.

Coming from the Epstein (just over the hill), your mind is on hands. Note how the Queen seems to twist her wedding ring in her lap : how can she trust the peaceful scene before her ? The King rests one clawlike hand on his lap ; but the other – large and flat as a shovel – is hidden from her ; spread on the outside of their makeshift throne. Thus, he braces himself erect – a bulwark for his Queen and his kingdom.

And true, as seasons pass, and elsewhere, other cities burn, it's you, who come to look, who are changing.

3. Dry Stane Dyke

At the top of the twisting road
leading out of Glenkiln, please stop.

(You're going to have to anyway,
to argue whose will be the job

of opening the cattle grid gate.)
Before you the Galloway hills

fan out across the horizon.
Follow each green peak, till your eye falls

to your right, to a bare, gently
sloping hillside, where a stone dyke

snakes its headless way, like a line
Paul Klee has taken for a walk

or a child's lassoo that's missed all
but one cloud-shadow and two trees

and lies in bracken abandoned.
Surely, no lawyer drew up deeds

to protect what's here, to deny
what isn't; surely those who laboured

with rock upon rock upon rock
up the hillside, didn't favour

these distant curves for their own sake.
Brecht has pointed out History

records only the names of kings
as Thebes' builders – a mystery

how *they* hauled so many great lumps
of rock! Neither instigator

nor workers are remembered here,
on wall plaque, stone or fine paper;

yet that kink at the far right end,
a lazy toe might improvise,

makes a mouth, that gives the whole
a fish-iness, that to my eyes

more than song, arch or tower, tells
of the playfulness of power.

4. Routin Linn

A bridge over water,
white water –
the Old Water
on its way to the Cluden.
The Old Water
tumbling through moss-
covered rock –
the Old Water
on its way to the Nith.
One zig
and one zag
through a glacial crack
and the Old Water's
on its way
to the Solway.

But here
and now
at Routin Linn,
that water –
the Old Water –
hits a brown,
wrinkled pool,
as a white fist
an open palm.

And the message?
What message?
The perception?
None.

Just be
with me
on this shoulder of rock
below the Brig.
From a rich wood
of hazel, birch
and alder, watch
through the arch
the white waters
fall.
          Yes and tell,
should you spot
a dipper end-
lessly bobbing
on a knuckle of rock
between two
white weaves
of water, its breast
such a fresh,
white splash !

5. The Twelve Apostles

(At Holywood – the largest stone circle on the Scottish mainland.)

'The Twelve' are eleven : four, giant boulders,
but seven quarried – and hauled here – from the living rock.
It's late when we pass them and easy to miss them
behind the thick hedge ; but, at the first toppled tomb
of whinstone glimpsed through the gate, you shoulder
time aside and seek out the other ten blocks.

Some pinion the damp earth ; others stand. All bear
livid scars of lava or are encrusted
with colonies of pale crystals. Stars of lichen
spatter the stone, nurtured by the innocent air.
An ash-grey time-hoard, their mean growth has been likened
to the stones' genesis – a formation entrusted

to another world of inexorable, patient pressures.
One, the first fish nuzzled as a floor of grit,
before plates of ice rolled it, in cold fury
stripping the lush glen bare. Another erupted
to burn holes through ten thousand nights. But what measure
do we have to hold their explosive histories,

to mine their hidden depths ? Darkening shadows stretch
from each earthfast menhir – huge cones that hurtled down
from a Silurian tree and never bore fruit.
Stand at each altar : you'll meet a spirit unmatched
by the green schools of grass, hedges, trees that surround
this oval of stones on the last leg of our route.

For all the budding world around them seems possible
to own. By deed or conquest, it changed hands.
(Even the gently flowing Cluden is divided
into stretches which come with someone's private lands.)
But the *gravitas* of the eleven 'Apostles'
disdains stewardship ; the tolerance provided

by every Kilness farmer who's bent a furrow
round them. They are not churches with crumbling towers :
their preservation does not praise us. And nor does
the gap-toothed hawthorn hedge, which divides them now –
four in one field, seven in the other – lose
them dignity or diminish their power.

Your eyes flit over the last, long diameters,
along sight-lines of rugged stone. Neither nature
nor art, but a power that draws each white-faced farm
within its compass. And you – till you hear the buzz
of traffic hitting a straight at last ; and the fuss
of the parallel world once more tugs at your arm.

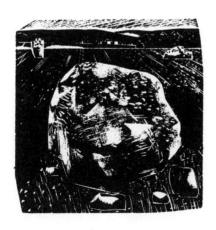

SECTION THREE

The Moth Trap

In the centre of the sloping lawn, light
from a moth-trap floods the garden – surreal,
as if thought walked a green ceiling and sight
in such strangeness became a matter of feel.

The cut-out trees, the black teeth of a fence
mark the limits of this ordered landscape;
gleaming on the horizon its last defence –
the even lights of a runway, roped

across the night. Two fat poplar hawks thud
dully against glass along with a smirr
of lesser life: creatures not of blood
or substance, their death – a silvery smere.

A meagre haul this, till two boys tilt
into light, to match elastic shadows
and faces white as saucers of milk.
Each new element they dive in draws

a measure of proof. And so we observe
one the light calms, the other light excites;
one's a campfire Indian, the other's nerves
are taut, conscious of the wider night.

The light gives his naked movements the grace
of a wild boy reared on the forest floor.
Clothing them with laughter, he lifts his face –
there is nothing yet that can't be shared.

'Isn't childhood . . . ?' But I have answered yes
before you finish, still feeling the impress
of something wounded but wonderful,
beating inside me against the darkness.

Portrait (Aged 6): Inverleith Park Pond

I

The V-neck he wears
(a light speckled blue),
over a striped T-shirt,
has been tucked into

the simple waist-band
of rucked, cotton shorts,
which reach his pale knock-knees.
There (with grey, school socks),

the photograph ends.
His right hand bunches
round a string attached
to a jam-jar. Much as

its contents must please,
he holds it away;
being mindful of
the jar – or jersey?

You can see pondweed
curl in on itself:
in its veined shadows,
the pencil-thick skelf

of a bright minnow.
The sun lights one side
of his face, but sharp,
dark shadows describe

the other. You sense
the softness of young skin,
feel the slight roughness
he feels when woollens

meet the bare forearms,
tighten round the legs.
His top lip sticks out
in a way that begs

questions : a childish
pout. And his eyes look
neither at camera
nor jar, but are locked

on something that can-
not be anything
other than *away*.
To the love that strung

the jam-jar, put him
on the edge of the pond,
folded the cuffs back
(and knitted them – by hand),

perhaps held his wrists,
as he scooped the net
through barely rippling
waters and yet let

him the final sweep,
this is his answer :
'Boy with a Minnow'.
He, himself, is elsewhere.

II

Mental arithmetic
was my nightmare.
I clung to my desk
in panic and stared

at stockades of knots
from which all meaning
had fled. The other side
of the wall – keening

softly – if only
I would trust the swim
of my intelligence
and break through their thin

cabbala, I sensed
I'd be in a sea
of faith, where the future
at last flowed freely.

But the dread numbers
kept coming – great cairns,
they pinioned the tip
of my tongue-tied brain.

In this stilted pose –
'Boy with a Minnow' –
the sun rolled round his
conscientious frown

I read the early
muddied stirrings of
such an arithmetic
the adult's made of love.

The left hand hangs limp,
awkward at his side ;
the pudgy fingers
parody *David*,

as they cup around
their shadowy stones.
Time is Goliath
between us – demons

dance at his shoulders.
I lift my left hand :
Love, hurtle through time –
free this boy of mine.

III

I feel the spring sun
warm on my back, catch
the slightly fetid
whiff of the pond ; watch

the gentlest ripples
washing an edge of
dead flies and litter.
From the verge above,

I look on a boy
caught stiffly posing
for a camera shot.
Does the sun cause him

to turn this way ? –
the veil of shyness
between us a sign
neither one's at ease

with strangers. But hold –
each chance encounter's
a question of choice :
so, before I falter,

I force an approach.
'What've you got there ?'
I ask, when I hear
the camera shutter.

The boy glances
at his father, then
at his mother, then
he places the jar

carefully, as if
it really is a prize,
back on its damp ring
of concrete. His eyes

are shining as I
pick it up, hold it
high against the sky.
Irridescent slits

of the gentlest green
arc round a silver
jewel – the water
itself is alive !

We all crowd round it –
the loving and loved,
the same – and we praise
this perfect world, gloved

in the simple jar
above us – our faces
now shadowless, bright
in the refracted light.

Snap

Hauntingly familiar, a picture
I found in the gutter of a strange girl
lying on a garishly striped sun-bed;
her bikini'd pose before the bright god
of the lens that mixture of starlet
and laughing unease that's the safest bet
these days in matters of self-exposure.
Her body, with the one raised thigh lowered
over the other, speaks of a common desire,
yet that you-devil-you look is lure
for what cameramen alone can share –
a secretive look that says: *remember*

how deep is skin deep; what our bodies know
is greater than they seek. Once sowed,
senses grow shoots into far tomorrows,
where it becomes hard to say what was true.
One day this easy pose, this tossed-back hair
was all for you: memory has stored
its power. Look! What you could not love then
has waited, curled around its lonely song;
till it is released by a snapped picture
of an unknown girl – found in the gutter.

Once I Knew You

to appear where
it seemed most unlikely
for you to be – gliding over
tussocky grass in a field
you could not know.

Your white breasts glowed
– Minoan in the moonlight –
everywhere else you wore black.
Softly, you spoke of buds
and hedge-flowers –

shadows that nest
in the darkness. And I
stumbled after your thoughts, as light
briefly held them – and your eyes –
then moved on ;

and your eyes – liquid
as the cows you moved through –
played with meaning ; turned me into
a Chagal dog, barking
at the simple moon.

Often, passing
the timid beasts of night,
I would feel a hum of need rise
in my throat like a thick croak.
Each of these toads

you took from me
and set down in the moonlight.
'There is the stuff of what gives you
your fear. Now help these creatures
find water.'

Side by side, we
stood on a rickety bridge
that, in the thin dawn light, hovered
over the slight river.
You pointed to

the bull-rushes
that clustered there : 'The will
has such elegance – when it is
exercised and strong.'
While below us,

the world turned
its face from happiness ;
turned also from despair : 'Somewhere,
down there' – and you pointed
to the dark tangle

of water and weed –
'are our reflections.'
Our love was a way of seeing.
It lives ; though you do not
come to me now.

Frogs

Like someone strapped to a *life* buoy,
you lead me to the cottage door.
'Are you sure you'll be all right?
I must have a torch somewhere.'

I see the path by the hall-light,
middling-muddy in falling rain;
the gate a gap in the broad hedge.
I grope my way, call out, 'I'm fine.'

Halfway to the gate already,
with our last goodnights, the faint light
of the kitchen window guides me
to where darkness seems complete –

the farm-track that leads to the road.
Here everything growing is black:
the central spine of tufted grass,
the hedge-wall, the cut-out trees flocked

with glimmering drops of rain.
The earth I walk on seems almost
metallic – a thin strip reaching
depths of darkness I cannot trust.

Yet the black is not so black,
when I recall the embers of haws,
the bright, wet coals of blackberry
this blind hedge, in daytime, grows.

And I feel, glowing within me,
the world I have left: the warm fire
of yet another receptive house,
where Alex, with bright purple hair,

drains the last of the berry-red wine
and laughs as she paints us her life ;
while Evan wraps himself in a book
and you smile through old pain and new love.

Easy to be there, to talk through –
with intelligence and feeling –
all the losses we need to grow ;
so that, in time, the precious few

unmuddied thoughts I have seem huge.
Later, driving home on the twisting roads,
my headlights catch tiny wet frogs,
leaping like electrified pods

of seaweed over black tarmac,
as though their short lives are at stake.
And I have it ! that breathless excitement –
the world before its waters break.

First Rites

Once again, it is the first night
of some good thing. Yet in this room
        sleep still can't know it –
sidling through, cagey as the moon :
at best we'll meet her at first light.

Till then, we lie in the darkness,
each, in thought, knowing the other's
        sleeplessness, yet holding
to stillness beneath the covers,
lest a brute world of feeling press

in and crush us. This is what I
am thinking (a thought the slight wind
        through the scaffolding
of trees has given me – the wind
which falls with a liquid sigh) :

if I can't have sleep, then let me
have rain. I want to hear the rain.
        At first, a few drops
and then, those same few drops again,
till someone turns a giant key

and the heavens open. No blame
for you in this, my love : my ways
        are mysterious
(or weird) to us both. But come, let's praise
the rain ; on this first night, it might tame

our just unease. For, with early light,
a darker awakening comes
        with a stag battering
his antlers against the wire drum
of the fence ; the finger-tips bright

with blood – an angry stain, which spreads
over them, till the fence itself
      bears a thin, red shield.
Never will he see his true wealth
through our eyes ; so why watch him wed

his beauty to violence
till dirty rags of skin hang down
      – softest velveteen –
draped each side of his bloody crown
and the fence rings in the silence ?

One of the Beaten, you'd think, now
he slams into the wire once more ;
      yet something in him knows
where he is going, that the gore
is but a blessing on his brow –

is where his strength has been planted.
As we watch, he and the blood-light
      of our geraniums
blur. A red tinge edges our night,
till a key turns and a wish is granted.

The Flower

I find you gone –
as you said you would – a walk
alone in the early morning
and to get a paper. Strange then –
in this, your first absence –
not to be thinking
of complications ; to pose
the testing questions : *How
exactly do you feel ? What's
the next move from here ?*

Or to rise from this crumpled bed
and pad, bare-foot,
catlike around each
empty room, breathing
easy, as your postcards
and toilet bag lie
open-mouthed before me.

Such thoughts would make
you shake your head.
'Funny man, you are.
Funny man.' Yes,
just lying here, arms
akimbo, sensing
my life hum in the silence.

I picture your busy
clockwork walk
round the still coves.
The silver water barely
ripples, as you launch the first
hopeful skiffy stone
into the bay. Two skips
and all human warmth
is washed from it. Memory
too has done with it. (But when
you stoop to recall
yesterday's names
of tormentil and thrift,
the red-tipped claw
of bird's foot trefoil
snags on your mind.)

And now I almost feel it –
your hair falling in my face
when you bring me coffee,
a paper and a wildflower
that's new to us both.

It is that moment I wish
I could hold to : the unnamed
flower between us,
turning in my fingertips,
washed by our mingled breaths –
a room for our eyes to live in.

How close
will we get
to this flower
before it burns
like any other
patch of colour?
Here, let it
turn in our eyes'
thirst to know it
as it now is
in all its fragile
delicacy,
its short-lived
perfection.
     And turn
one more time,
before I reach
for the book to name it –
if it should have a name –
and you take it
and carefully
place it
and press it.

The Moth

Along the verge of a lochside track,
my eye falls on a dead bramble leaf,
its dun colours misplaced amidst the life
of green that, in late July, must fight

for air and earth room. And to this dead leaf,
another is joined – seam to impossible
seam. I look closer and my senses
thrill to the soft, rustling syllable

of a moth embossed with gold. Yes,
on each folded wing, giving the richest
camouflage of all – two flashes of purest,
beaten gold. I break off the leaf it sits on

and hold it to the light, which slants
through silver birches lining the path.
I only link stillness with life, when I spot
the ivory bead of an egg, funnelling

out of its sharp abdomen. I turn the stalk
between my fingers and the moth
revolves – precious as a jewel
from the treasure of Pharaohs.

Gold threads down its upper wings
and trailing from the great furry head
are two fine gold antennae sweeping back
the length of its bullet-shaped body.

Such oriental extravagance! We
have never seen the like.

Though there will be wonder in its migrant story,
the echoing halls of entymology
will grant it only the tiniest of pedestals.
But for us now, between its wing-folds,

a magic heart beats and we do not want
it named yet, do not want its trick of light
in any way explained. The wind has dropped,
as if the whole world holds its breath –

is propped on its ancient stick
and moving closer.

The Foxglove

(Source of the drug digitalis, *which is used to treat heart ailments.)*

I

Nothing tame about
the foxglove that grew
by that cottage stream.

More like a tall fir
or proud cyprus than
flower, but wild and

not waving, but swaying
its coat o' bells in strong
summer breezes. Once

it would have stood
no chance to stay
so tall : the hand

that stripped docken
and fingers of fern,
that waged open war

on all things taller
than grass, smaller than
a tree, with a good stick,

would have brought it
crashing down in a blur
of bruised and broken

blossoms – a panic
of feasting bees. (See
its stringy stalk still

joined by a few green
umbilicals – the rest
ruined, utterly.)

But it grew way past
the end of my growing,
my lust to see the tall

– in nature – fall.
Both its time and spot
were well-chosen.

II

A secret track leads
from the cottage door
to a short tumble

of water and a clear,
cool basin, now choked
with forbidding broom.

This lies just below
the ford,
        where years before,
the waters in spate,

the farmer made a bridge
of an old, broken
trailertop. The backboard

he cast aside
in tufted grass
to bloom with lice.

There it has weathered,
till the wood is grey
and mossed as rock –

a strength that lies ;
for through its broken back
the foxglove had thrust.

(What a clean swipe
it could have been !
I felt the shocked itch

of the limbless.)
        That week
in idle routine, I'd
walk over to peer

down a spotted throat,
past the lip of sparse,
white stubble, designed

to keep the needless
out. The yellow sacks
of pollen clustered

on the flower's roof,
fresh as morning rolls,
on the curving ends

of milky tendrils.
Or – thoughtfully – I'd
sleeve a few fingers

with any seamless,
lilac softness that
had already fallen.

The onion-domed
seedcases themselves,
fat and shining-green –

the point of the staff –
were waiting for time
and a little sun

to lean on them. The tip
of the foxglove curved –
a tender probe or

questionmark. Still,
even if I stood
at its base and shook

till I was buried
in all its blossoms,
what could that foxglove

tell, but of itself?
There have been nights
– far from it – when

I've dreamed I sit
on the rotting fibres
of that board and clutch

the foxglove like a mast.
The wind slaps leather-
leaves against me,

seedcases explode
at last above me;
yet I remain calm

for I have taken
the foxglove's medicine:
my heart grows strong

and I don't even wake
now, when I feel
the deep roots loosening.

Message

Typing a poem
    a final draft – the usual
        excited way

my brain – stalled
    over the v – watches
        as my fingertip

too late, comes
    lightly down
        on the f. So

what I have
    isn't the 'leaving'
        my quick fingers

would have, by now
    completed, but 'leaf'
        with that ghostly

trailed f. Not
    'leaving' but
        'leafing'. The word

drops into my mind
    like a feather
        or a leaf.

And another.
    And again
        another.

Leafings. All of them
    help the green buds
        grow tall

though we all
    must live a little
        in their shade.

Casey's

(Glandore, Co. Cork, looks over the bay and its islands – Adam and Eve.)

At last, as the creamy clouds of Guinness
slowly settled, he acknowledged that today
was a *bad* day. His face – a Barry Fitzgerald
of crumpled kindness – peered with us

at the drizzle filling the bay of Glandore.
The hazy wedges of Adam and Eve
were dark-grey smudges on the smudgy sea.
Yesterday – warmer, but with a mist thick

as a west Cork accent – we had stood
and stared out at a safety curtain
that had never risen on the day. 'Still,
not a bad day,' opined Larry Casey,

fourth generation owner of Casey's
three and a half centuries old bar; now
more given to tourists than fisherfolk.
That first night, Adam and Eve were sharp-edged

as anvils at the head of the bay.
'A mile apart,' Mr. Casey told us,
his tone assured of our quizzical 'No!'
'Yes. And once they used to lie side by side;

but since the terrible sin that cast us all
from Eden, God has made them ever lie
so far apart.' This told with a slight smile:
it was a gift of whose worth he was sure.

But when customers talked, Mr. Casey
withdrew to a quiet seat near the bar.
Snippets of conversation fell to him :
'Where there's children, there's life – don't you think?'

'Ah yes,' came the soft voice round the corner,
'tis lovely to be innocent.' The last night,
we talked of the Glandore Regatta.
'Tis a pity you're going, right enough –

tis a fine day, the Glandore Regatta.
Still, if you've got the time, you shouldn't miss
the view above Loch Ine. Yes, I tell all
the visitors about it, for it is –

to my way o' thinking – the most beautiful
spot in Ireland.' His small, guiding hands curved
round many roads ; spidered up the hillside.
'Here you can take a little rest. And here . . .'

While outside, only the sea mist hugged Eve,
as the sailing manuals told it, and the rain
– that tireless step-dancer – kept on trying
to douse ten thousand beams of fuschia.

On Arran

Five deer, we'd thought
fenced-in with sheep,
tamed with lush, lowland grass,

within reach of hawthorns
and the sea, appear on the road
and, from a standing jump, flow

over the wire fence
into the opposite field,
into a contrary landscape,

like water poured
from one glass into another.
By the time we've locked the car

and got over the stile,
someone's moved them way up
the green hillside. They stand

close, but too neatly –
a giveaway grouping – arranged
by some childish, godlike hand.

Then we are two parties –
the two parties of the glen –
they always a little higher,

a little ahead, vaulting
through the landscape, not even
touching the heather; as we,

contrary beings, it seems
seep with each new step
further into a banking of mud

and sedge smoothed flat
after a full winter's wet.
They stop now and stare us out

across the mountain stream.
Sniffing, their elegant heads
assume a natural aristocracy ;

while we, clumsy but bright
savants of the mountains,
wave and shout them on :

'You've come thus far ;
now we are the life –
the life of Glean Easan Biorach

and you must stay with us –
at least to the cold, blue heart
of Loch na Davie, to the very edge

of the grey mist rolling
down Cir Mhor. We seek signs
of companionship, not judgement.'

  • • • •

We scour the hillside,
but they've become so many
heathery streaks between scree.

Of course, I think that later.
For the moment, I stand with you,
coated in the soft, island rain,

and stare and stare
over the empty, glacial valley,
till you say, 'Well, can you

spot them then ? Can you ?'
But what is there to answer you
that is not root, water or rock ?

On Saddleworth

(The search for the long-dead victims of the Moors murders.)

The world is old.
*It seemed older
twenty years ago.*

The moors are cold.
*They were colder
twenty years ago.*

Will horror unfold?
*It did so
twenty years ago.*

To what can we hold?
*There was nothing
twenty years ago*

*when blood ran cold
and got colder. It was
twenty years ago.*

SECTION FOUR

SECTION FOUR

Visiting the Poet

(After Akhmatova's tribute to Aleksandr Blok.)

When I visit the poet,
when is not important.
It's the same firm handshake;
then whisky, water and glasses.

The city can be grey and cold;
his walls are stoked against it:
landscapes, friends; spines/spines/spines
and flame-haired faces.

My host is never silent for long –
interrupts with a look
if my language is loose: for his talk
is as honed as his writing.

I remember a conversation
we had once. I wrote it down later.
Like most of our talks,
it concerned poetry.

He told me: you must have faith
that there's water in the well;
trust your ear; pick up a pen
at the slightest nudging.

And lastly – hours or minutes
from my arrival – he told me:
'Remember this: you never know what
you may do tomorrow.'

Good advice, don't you think? –
even when set down on the cold page
without the warmth of whisky
or the conviction of a lifetime.

The Children of the Russian Fair

I

This morning huge pale toadstools poke
through the rivermist. Once again the tents and the awnings.
Can it be a year already ? A whole year ? And so soon
that I must face their children again ?

Dribbling in loud and late over the frozen fields
yet still arriving muddy, they refuse all correction –
the closest to contrition, when they huddle before me,
muttering darkly, averting sullen, sexless faces.
It's then I catch it – their air of sour-sweet
animal ordure, of thick blue grease and cold sweat.

On Friday afternoons, at their worst, they fidget
interminably ; swivelling round on already polished pants,
winding themselves up (I suppose) for the roundabouts
they must take command of come night – threading their way
between fantastical seats with feline agility –
never missing a kopek.

'Is there something wrong with you,' I address
the darkening room, 'that you find it
impossible to sit still ?'

II

The slow fizz of their bottled mirth hits me long before
I have finished and they have turned to each other –
even the quietest – drenching the room with laughter.
'Did you hear that?' they shout. 'Did you hear that?'

And they are off, clambering through the broken slats;
trampling all my beloved young seedlings back
into the mire: or whirling torn images around themselves –
little dervishes, their chiffon head-dresses catching
the last of the winter light. The room echoes
as they dunt each stricken metaphor to see
where it can most easily be broken.

Like a distant uncle, who by sheer chance
has stumbled on the perfect gift, I almost love them now,
as I watch them skip away into the dark November evening –
back to the mechanical poetry of roundabouts,
to mongrel puppies and rancid stews.

Their delighted chant still warms them:
'Did you hear him? Did you hear him?
Kak krasnaya krasnaya rosa.
Kak krasnaya rosa.' Crows flapping
in a winter landscape – 'kak kak kak.'

Russian Still-Life

(Kiev-to-Moscow sleeper.)

Though the signs are of sleep,
neither one of us has slept.
The rocking train has kept
us awake, till pale light seeps
through the rucked blue curtains.
Both our pillows lie crushed,
points twisted in a rush
of anger. But nothing gained
ignoring day, we've pulled
at half the blue and swiped
our damp breath away. Light
from the orange sun – cool
as Vermeer – paints the rims
of tea-glasses silver,
makes a spoon's tip quiver.
Four tea-bags weep in the dim
of the saucer, like dank,
old leaves. Augurs of day:
your rolled tie; the way
that towel offers its blank
image, waiting for a face.
Tall birch trees shimmer past.
Lit from behind, they mask
great fields that show no trace
of all the blood that made them.
They are ploughed silences –
the horizons their fence.
And, before the station's mayhem,
I note this last down:
flowers in a curved vase,
whose small heads are scraps of lace
torn from the fading moon.

Kissing a Hand in Chekhov

I am kissing a hand in Chekhov.
Above me her face is already a memory,
a watery glow in the evening light.
(And she too, poor dear, a student of meanings.)

I am kissing a hand in Chekhov.
Beyond this room : an estate, a forest,
a distance that runs into silence. Listen :
the clock, the horse bells' slight impatience.

I am kissing a hand in Chekhov.
Already, think of it, past her white breasts,
the shimmer of lace. And still I bend,
displacing air into the endless tedium.

I am kissing a hand in Chekhov,
holding her fingers like delicate pods
that might split at the merest pressure –
or else break out into flame.

I am kissing a hand in Chekhov.
Ergo, I am learning how to lose.